A Praise the Lord series book

Thank You Lord

... for all life's circumstances...

Change your outlook on life!

By Michelle Lovato

Thank You, Lord

Boutique Books

Thank You, Lord

For all life's circumstances...

Change your outlook on life

By Michelle Lovato

Thank You!

Thank You, Lord for this fabulous life you gave me that is full of problems and problem people. There are also dozens of precious people as well and I am blessed to have learned from their knowledge, benefited from their mistakes and enjoyed their lives with them.

Thank you Vince Lovato for mentoring excellent writing skills and providing a life-time supply of love. Thank you my children for enabling me to look to our Father in Heaven for advice, guidance and rest.

Thank you women mentors whom I've walked with in church and non-church settings through the years who taught me the Biblical concepts of Godly women.

Thank you Pastors Allen Barnes, Terry Morrow, Rueben Gomez and Ed Clements for sharing the deep places of God with me. Thank you Jeff Krausman for your constant dedication to prayer.

Thank you Michael Hyatt for realizing so many like me have a message from God to share and teaching us how to share them.

- Michelle Lovato

Thank you, Lord is dedicated to my family, who
continue to encourage me to use the gifts
God gave me to their fullest.

Thank you, Vince,
Melissa, Shawn, Reagan, Carter,
Christian, Brandie and Jeremy.
I adore every one of you.

Note from the author

    I began my relationship with our Lord Jesus Christ on July 11, 1979 while at a youth concert at Calvery Chapel in Costa Mesa, CA.

    That night the single most important event of my life occurred because I found the answer to how I would stack one day upon another to journey through this difficult life. As I read my Bible and prayed to God, he blessed me with a sense of peace and happiness that now defines who I am. My life was, and still is, jammed packed with stress, instability and the constant bitter influence of the evil one trying to destroy me. But I can still smile. The Lord is my friend and I am so thankful I don't walk through life alone.

- Michelle Lovato

Thank You, Lord

Foreword

Thank You Lord is a gift book and journal for busy readers and is focused on looking at life's bad situations as opportunities to grow closer to God.

Every page offers readers another chance to redirect negative life experiences into a conscious leaning closer to God, who is able to supply you joy when trial persist.

> Be joyful in hope, patient in affliction, faithful in prayer.
>
> Romans 12:12 (NIV)

We humans were never designed to be without the presence of God. But because of sin and its persistent moment-by-moment intrusion in our lives, realizing Godly joy comes only after we choose a close one-on-one relationship with God.

> Remain in me, as I also remain in you. No branch can bear fruit by itself; it must remain in the vine. Neither can you bear fruit unless you remain in me.
>
> I have told you this so that my joy may be in you and that your joy may be complete.
>
> John 15: 4, 11 (NIV)

Michelle Lovato

Joy is the product of God's open-armed invitation and exists in every situation. It is Christ in you.

Use Thank You, Lord to seek joy when your life isn't going exactly how you hoped and make it a moment-by-moment part of your life.

Draw close to God in praise and watch him share his love with you.

> But the fruit of the Spirit is love, joy,
> peace, forbearance, kindness, goodness,
> faithfulness, gentleness, self control.
>   Galatians 5:22, 23a

- Michelle

Thank You, Lord

How to use this book

Let your words be a praise to God Almighty who Knows your heart and wants your committed life. Sit down daily and make it a point to read one praise, then create your own. I believe with all my heart that if you do, God will be pleased.

O Lord, you have searched me and you Know me. You Know when I sit and when I rise; you perceive my thoughts from afar.

You discern my going out and my lying down; you are familiar with all my ways.

Before a word is on my tongue you Know it completely, O Lord.

Psalm 139: 1-4 (NIV)

Thank You, Lord

Month 1

Thank You, Lord today...

Thank you Lord for defining everything that is good in my life. Thank you for turning my daily problems into chances to serve you, chances to grow closer to you and chances to grow closer to those around me.

I love you Lord every moment of the day even when those moments are filled with sorrow. I am alive in you.

Thank You, Lord that you are concerned with my spiritual well being so much that You sent Your son to die for me.

I love You, Lord.

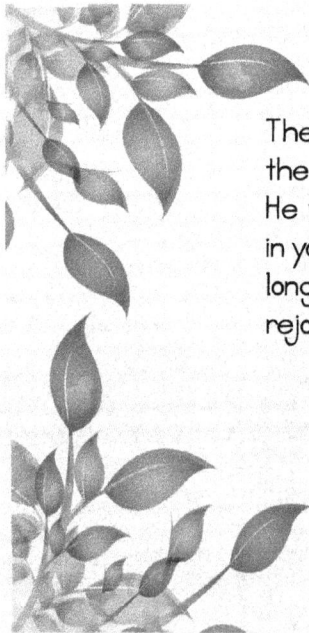

The Lord your God is with you,
the Mighty Warrior who saves.
He will take great delight
in you; in his love he will no
longer rebuke you, but will
rejoice over you with singing.
Zephaniah 3:17 (NIV)

Thank You, Lord

Thank You, Lord today...

Thank You, Lord today...

Thank You, Lord for giving me my husband who is my dearest friend, my closest ally my go-to guy when I need a break. Even when he ignores the housework and fails to cook when I am at work, he is my hero and thank you for reminding me that pizza can be delivered.

Thank You for my kids who compel me to feel unexplainable joy, astounding embarrassment, brain-swelling frustration and happiness beyond any compare. Thank You that they misbehave, stand on my shoes, pull on my arms and beg for my attention.

Thank You that the gift of their child-like wonder never ends, because it is through them that you teach me how to be patient and loving.

●——●ॐ●——●

Behold, children are a heritage from the Lord,
the fruit of the womb a reward.
Psalm 127:3 (ESV)

Thank You, Lord

Thank You, Lord today...

47

Thank You, Lord today...

Heavenly Lord, ruler of all moments in time, you are the beginning and the end. You define birth, life, infinity and eternity. I love you.

Thank you for allowing so many disturbing challenges in my life. Though 'Life Happens,' thank you for allowing me to find you, your mercy and love. Those hard times teach me to turn to you. I love your way. How I love your perfect will.

Thank you for using my flawed life as your tool and teaching me that abundant life is found by following you. Thank you for walking through this journey with me. I love you Lord.

Take delight in the Lord, and he will give you the desires of your heart.
Psalm 37:4 (NIV)

Thank You, Lord

Thank You, Lord today...

Thank You, Lord today...

Thank you, Lord, for allowing me to feel grief in losing bad habits because after the cravings are gone, I realize that it shapes me into a stronger servant. I'm not fond of letting go of my hidden desires even when I know they are not Godly. My human side wants the worldy. Thank you that though I don't understand your plan, I know you are in control of my today, tomorrow and eternity.

Thank you Lord for sending me comfort through your sons and daughters and thank you that no devastation I face is more powerful than you.

Thank you Lord that your Word holds the answer to all my prayers and that the Holy Spirit moves me through my interaction. I love you Lord.

Remember your word to your servant, in which you have made me hope. This is my comfort in my affliction, that your promise gives me life. The insolent utterly deride me, but I do not turn away from your law.
Psalm 119:49-51 (ESV)

Thank You, Lord

Thank You, Lord today...

Thank You, Lord today...

Thank you, Lord, today for giving your child another chance to rest in your heavenly arms. When I am distraught about my circumstances, or enjoying pure jubulation, you are ever present to guide me.

Thank you that your Holy Spirit wants to live in my heart, sweep out my cobwebs, walk with me and hold my hand.

Thank you that in you my future is assured, my eternity awaits, because you will continue to accompany me during every moment of my life.

Thank you for your renewed messages of encouragement and love through your Word.

I love you Lord.

You realize, don't you, that you are the temple of God, and God himself is present in you? No one will get by with vandalizing God's temple, you can be sure of that. God's temple is sacred and you, remember, are the temple.

1 Corinthians 3:16-17 (MSG)

Thank You, Lord today...

Thank You, Lord today...

Thank you Lord for gifting me with boundless energy, a healthy dose of patience, a somewhat distorted idea of organization and tolerance for those whom I annoy.

I love you Lord for understanding how strenuous raising a family can be. It is like living onboard a pirate ship full of swashbuckling crew members ready to mutiny.

Thank you for equipping me to handle it all. Thank for all the new ideas you give me everyday to entertain and teach my kids in the ways you want them to go. Thank you for allowing me to be your servant and for the ability to quell their sometimes mutinous hearts. I love you Lord.

Out of my distress I called on the Lord; the Lord answered me and set me free. The Lord is on my side; not fear. What can man do to me?
Psalm 118:5-6
(ESV)

Thank You, Lord

Thank You, Lord today...

Thank You, Lord today...

Thank you Lord for giving me my unique and valuable life.

Thank you that you made me with a special set of talents that you planned all along to utilize for your kingdom.

Thank you for overwhelming me with chores and jobs and the secret longing to play. It is in those experiences that I learn how to handle the many responsibilities and blessings you have in store for me.

I love your great foresight, knowledge and majesty. I love your ways.

Thank you Lord for your interaction in my daily world.

I love you.

Every good gift and every perfect gift is from above, coming down from the Father of lights with whom there is no variation or shadow due to change.

James 1:17 (ESV)

Thank You, Lord

Thank You, Lord today...

Thank You, Lord today...

Thank you Lord for rescuing me from my evil human will, my self-centered, egotistical will.

Your glory and perfect plan stand out against my own foolish decisions. You repair my life again and again.

Thank you Lord that you know my heart when I do not know it myself, for keeping your rescue net close at hand, ready to catch me each time I begin to flutter away from your path.

I am embarassed by my stubborn intent to sin, but Lord thank you for re-capturing my heart. Thank you Lord that you continue to wait for me. You are insatiable in your pursuit of me every minute of my life.

Thank you Lord.

So cut away the thick calluses from your heart and stop being so willfully hardheaded. God, your God, is the God of all gods, he's the Master of all masters, a God immense and powerful and awesome.
Deuteronomy 16-17 (MSG)

28

Thank You, Lord today...

Thank You, Lord today...

Thank you Lord for giving me yet another hairy-week. There are so many things to do and never enough time to do them all. Thank you that I learned this week to turn to you for help. Even the smallest things, like sleep, came at the whisper of your blessing.

Thank you for many long hours running, running, running through life and the welcome relief when I drop onto the couch with a cool drink, too overwhelmed with fatigue to continue.

Thank you for the excitement of activity and the rush of adrenaline that accompanies every task. Thank you for a sense of completion when my list is done and the constant reminder that another list waits for tomorrow, along with your well of plentiful mercy and grace ready for me to drink.

I love you Lord.

Give thanks to the Lord,
for he is good! His faithful
love endures forever.
Psalm 136:2 (NIV)

Thank You, Lord

Thank You, Lord today...

Thank You, Lord today...

Thank you Lord for standing close to me. My heart is grimy, my life and my past are dark with sin, rancid with choices I made without you.

Thank you for plugging your nose, breaking out the soap and washing my heart clean of my seemingly unforgivable actions.

Thank you Lord for loving the unworthy, boastful, self-motivated, needy me. I do not understand the depth of love you feel for me, or the commitment you made, thank you for saving my life.

Lord, thank you that through your example in Jesus, you teach me how to love others who are just like me.

I love you.

Come now, let us settle the matter, says the LORD. Though your sins are like scarlet, they shall be as white as snow; though they are red as crimson, they shall be like wool.

Isaiah 1:18

Thank You, Lord

Thank You, Lord today...

Thank You, Lord today...

Thank you Lord for the joy you put in my heart when I am at my wits end. You are my rock when my anxious days go haywire and my entertainment when you make crazy bad things into good.

Thank you that I started my first day at work, breathless and terrified that I was late and learned I was actually six hours early. Thank you for my new day-shift friends and those I met during night shift. Thank you that they laughed at me. Now they know me by name and smile every shift-change when we meet.

Thank you for overlooking my weakness and exhibiting yourself through me. I love the way you work. I love you Lord.

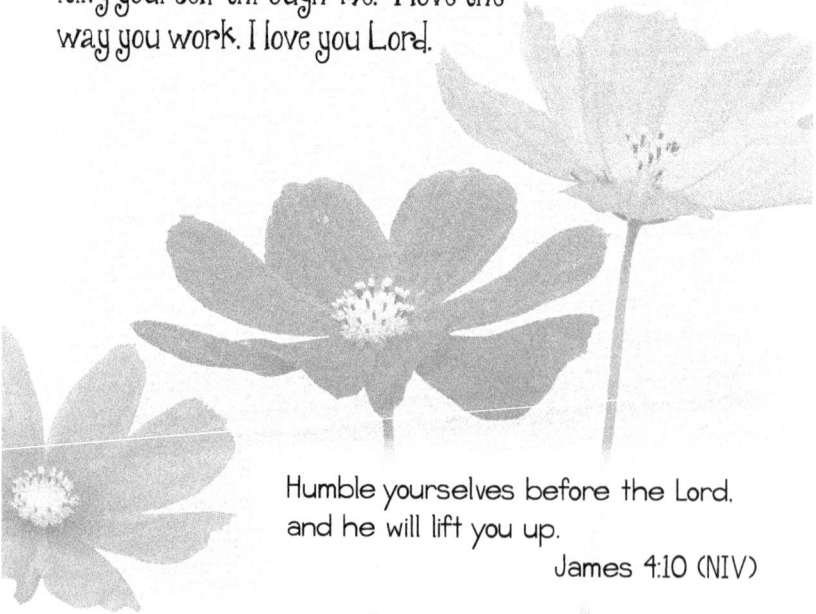

Humble yourselves before the Lord,
and he will lift you up.

James 4:10 (NIV)

Thank You, Lord

Thank You, Lord today...

Michelle Lovato

Thank You, Lord today...

Heavenly father I love you.

Thank you that you are my warm hug in times of fear, my stern guidance counselor when indecision plagues me. You greet me at the beginnng, the end and during every moment of my day to provide me what I need rather than what I want.

When you say 'no' I learn to accept that some things I want are not what you know I need.

My heart longs to beat in accordance with you. Praise you and thank you for hearing me call. Praise you and thank you for running to my side. Praise you and thank you for holding my hand. Praise you and thank you Lord for never giving up on me.

I love you Lord.

And whatever you do, whether in word or deed, do it all in the name of the Lord Jesus, giving thanks to God the Father through him.

Colossians 3:17 (NIV)

Thank You, Lord today...

Thank You, Lord today...

Thank you Lord for reminding
me today that you are patiently
waiting for me to communi-
cate with you.
Thank you for the
medium of prayer; for
guidelines and free-
form expression of my
desire to share heart-
to-heart talks with
you. I am content when
intimate with you in my
heart.
Praise you for the won-
derful time we share through
prayer; talking my heart out,
listening to your beautiful message,
hearing your angels sing sweet songs of salvation and
praise. Thank you for being my God. I love your nature.
I love you Lord.

───•✠•───

Therefore, since we have been justified
through faith, we have peace with God
through our Lord Jesus Christ.

Romans 5:1 (NIV)

Thank You, Lord today...

Thank You, Lord today...

Thank you Lord for quieting my voice, calming my heart and offering me a chance to listen.

It is a gift of unmeasurable size and requires me to stop thinking about myself and focus on you.

Thank you that your love is so simple and yet so terribly profound. Your glory humbles me and your righteousness brings me to my knees.

And yet you are so gentle with my foibles, with the things I do that dissapoint you, that dissapoint my family and friends.

Thank you for handling me with care.

I love you Lord.

Look carefully then how you walk, not as unwise but as wise.
Ephesians 5:15 (ESV)

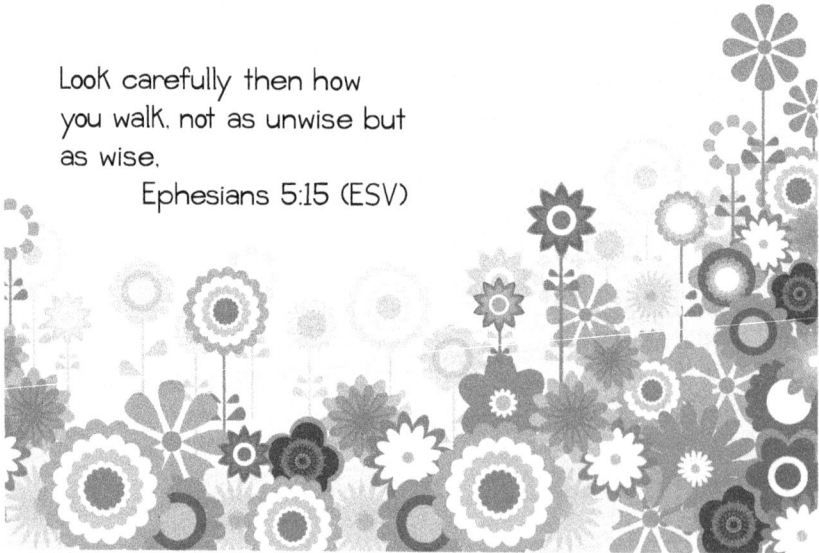

Thank You, Lord

Thank You, Lord today...

Michelle Lovato

Thank You, Lord today...

Thank you Lord for helping me traverse the narrow road toward your mighty kingdom.

Thank you for good walking boots, an abundance of supplies and the tackle necessary to trapes, trudge and triumph through the journey you have set forth.

I love it that walking on your path might take me around the globe or across the street and into my neighbor's yard. Your path makes every day significant, it is a chance to make my life matter for your perfect will.

Thank you for your Holy Word.

It lights the path of your awesome vision for me.

You are so beautiful Lord.

Thank you for making me beautiful in you.

I love you Lord.

Arise, walk about the land through its length and breadth: for I will give it to you.

Genesis 13:17 (NASB)

Thank You, Lord

Thank You, Lord today...

Thank You, Lord today...

Thank you Lord for the boundless energy you have blessed me with today! Thank you that you provided enough pep to leap through the morning, jump through the afternoon and zoom through the evening.

Thank you that you provide the zip for my zap and put the pop in my pep.

Thank you Lord for healing my body from the little pains for which it ails.

Thank you that you have restored my health and vitality so that I may bow down and serve your Holy name.

I love you Lord.

Therefore, as you received Christ Jesus the Lord, so walk in him.
Colossians 2:6 (ESV)

Thank You, Lord

Thank You, Lord today...

Michelle Lovato

Thank You, Lord today...

Thank you Lord that you never betray me.

You alone are the One True God, Omniscient Deity, Lord of All Creation.

There are so many things I do not understand. Thank you that I am a simple human, made in your likeness and loved by you.

Thank you that in my confusion about your wonders, that you are absolutely sure about my next step and can lead me down your path.

Thank you Lord for sending your son Jesus to be both God and human. It seems like such a far-fetched idea. But you made it clear that Jesus came to die for our sins and reconnect humanity with you.

Thank you that you care so much about me, about all of us, that you would create the opportunity to become reconnected.

I love you.

For God so loved the world that he gave his one and only Son, that whoever believes in him shall not perish but have eternal life.

John 3:16 (NIV)

Thank You, Lord

Thank You, Lord today...

Michelle Lovato

Thank You, Lord today...

Thank you Lord for direction and focus on the things you have set aside just for me.

Thank you that I am never alone. Thank you that I can look to your face and find a smile, look to your heart and find forgiveness, look to your Word and find your will.

Thank you for the Holy Spirit's help allowing me to comprehend and appreciate you. Thank you for outrageous gift of your daily companionship.

> But the Advocate, the Holy Spirit, whom the Father will send in my name, will teach you all things and will remind you of everything I have said to you.
>
> John 14:26 (NIV)

Thank You, Lord

Thank You, Lord today...

Thank You, Lord today...

Thank you Lord for demanding my complete and utter faithfulness to you. I would not have made it past noon without falling into sin if you were not there to remind me..

Thank you that your love does not interact with evil. You are the light that shines from a hill.

Thank you that you cover me with your light and instruct me to shine it on someone else.

Thank you for loving me so much that when I feel a great burden on my heart, it is because you have put it in place so I can serve you through your Holy example.

Thank you that I can find in you the path you want me to follow.

I love you Lord.

For the Lord your God is a consuming fire, a jealous God.

Deuteronomy 4:24 (NIV)

Thank You, Lord

Thank You, Lord today...

Thank You, Lord today...

Thank you Lord today for strength and vision, power and love.

Thank you that when my life seems completely out of control, you are present and employ the Holy Spirit to petition you on my behalf, lead me forward in faith.

Thank you for giving me peace when everything around me exists in utter chaos.

Thank you that you never cease to stand by the side of your servants and friends. Thank you that I am both your servant and friend.

I love you Lord.

Greater love has no one than this: to lay down one's life for one's friends. You are my friends if you do what I command. I no longer call you servants, because a servant does not know his master's business. Instead, I have called you friends, for everything that I learned from my Father I have made known to you. You did not choose me, but I chose you and appointed you so that you might go and bear fruit; fruit that will last and so that whatever you ask in my name the Father will give you. This is my command: Love each other.

John 15:13-17 (NIV)

Thank You, Lord

Thank You, Lord today...

Thank You, Lord today...

Thank you Lord for being my constant and trusted friend. Sometimes I feel so terribly alone in my needs and when I can turn to you and I know you are beside me, my sorrow does not feel so deep. Thank you for your effortless commitment to being my rock-solid savior, my still-small voice and my ardent defender.

Thank You for the failures that nearly overwhelmed me today because when I gave those failures to you, you reformed my soul and re-energized my skill set. Your transforming grace showed me that I could get through another storm with you by my side.

I love you Lord.

Take my side. God. I'm getting kicked around, stomped on every day.
Not a day goes by but somebody beats me up: They make it their duty to beat me up.
When I get really afraid I come to you in trust.
I'm proud to praise God: fearless now. I trust in God.
What can mere mortals do?

Psalm 56:3-4 (MSG)

Thank You, Lord

Thank You, Lord today...

Thank You, Lord today...

Thank you Lord for showing me I've erred.

Even when I do not want to hear those words, Lord, thank you that you love me enough to deliver them.

Thank you that you forgive me and thank you that my family loves me enough to forgive me time and again.

Thank you that your kind-hearted redirection is done with love, tenderness and forgiveness.

I love you Lord for creating in me a clean heart.

I love you Lord.

For the moment all discipline seems painful rather than pleasant, but later it yields the peaceful fruit of righteousness to those who have been trained by it.

Hebrews 12:11 (ESV)

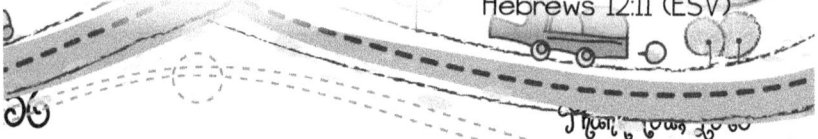

Thank You, Lord today...

Thank You, Lord today...

Thank you Lord for your repeated, patient forgiveness.

How I must exhaust you with all my un-learned lessons and yet you are tenacious in your persistent attention to me. You care about me. Truly care.

Thank you for being who you are. Thank you Lord that though I have defiled myself through sin and I am ashamed to look toward your heavenly face, you still call after me.

Thank you that you are present, here with me, that you called me in my past.

I love you.

For the word of God is living and active, sharper than any two-edged sword, piercing to the division of soul and of spirit, of joints and of marrow, and discerning the thoughts and intentions of the heart.

Hebrews 4:12 (ESV)

Thank You, Lord

Thank You, Lord today...

Thank You, Lord today...

Thank you Lord that you are beside me when I wander into fields of isolation, loneliness, despair and grief. There are days when I feel so alone that I am overcome by fatigue and want nothing more than to sleep the day away.

Yet you are there for me. If I ask for your help, you breathe peace into my heart.

Thank you for holding my hand. You are silently, softly, reassuringly Holy.

Thank you, Lord for being the still small voice that stubbornly yearns to talk to me after all these years and for being a great big God that watches my every move.

Thank you Lord for sheltering me from the hot sun of sin and for quenching my thirst when I am parched of you.

I love you, Lord.

Submit yourselves therefore to God. Resist the devil, and he will flee from you.
James 4:7 (ESV)

Thank You, Lord

Thank You, Lord today...

Thank You, Lord today...

Thank you Lord for laughing with me when I do silly things that make other people laugh along.

Thank you that you gave me a sense of confidence in you and a sense of humor that allows me to enjoy my quirkiness and know that I am not a hopeless lunatic.

Thank you that I can see in these moments of care-less abandon that others are entertained, that their days are lightened just a touch because they enjoyed a good laugh.

Thank you for all the comedy and comedians in my life.

I love you Lord.

A joyful heart is good
medicine, but a crushed
spirit dries up the bones.
        Proverbs 17:22 (ESV)

Thank You, Lord today...

Thank You, Lord today...

Thank you Lord for carrying me through another long day. I thought I wouldn't make it past lunch, but you had different plans.

Thank you that the car ran well, that the road remained safe, that the children remained calm...ish.

Thank you that there was money in the bank, food in the cupboards and peace in our family.

Thank you Lord that my husband did the laundry, the kids had towels and the bathroom had soap.

Thank you Lord for all your good gifts, generous blessings and your great love.

I love you Lord.

—•☸•—

If God gives such attention to the appearance of wildflowers most of which are never even seen don't you think he'll attend to you, take pride in you, do his best for you? What I'm trying to do here is to get you to relax, to not be so preoccupied with getting, so you can respond to God's giving. People who don't know God and the way he works fuss over these things, but you know both God and how he works. Steep your life in God-reality, God-initiative, God-provisions. Don't worry about missing out. You'll find all your everyday human concerns will be met.

Matthew 6:30-33 (MSG)

Thank You, Lord

Thank You, Lord today...

Thank You, Lord today...

Thank you Lord for teaching me good lessons.

Thank you that your swift and steady hand disciplines and reminds me that you are the God of the Universe and I am your child.

Thank you that I don't have to fear what I would do if you were not there because you promised in your Word you would never abandon me.

Thank you that you continue to walk through life with me, that you walk through life with all your children and you continue to call out to walk with those who are lost.

Thank you that your heart of love is so incredibly beautiful and forgiving.

I love you Lord.

When the poor and needy seek water, and there is none, and their tongue is parched with thirst, I the Lord will answer them; I the God of Israel will not forsake them.
Isaiah 41:17 (ESV)

Thank You, Lord

Thank You, Lord today...

Thank You, Lord today...

Thank you Lord for the life that abounds around me.
Its busyness keeps my mind racing and my heart
happy.
Its swirl puts a twirl in my skirt and in my heart.
The life you create makes my life sparkle.
Thank you that it inspires me to be well and to take
part in the activity that makes up my life.
Thank you that you are the Lord of good gifts and
bless me with such happiness and joy.
Thank you for the peace that passes understand.
I love you Lord.

———●———

I perceived that there is nothing better
for them than to be joyful and to do
good as long as they live.
                    Ecclesiastes 3:12 (ESV)

Thank You, Lord

Thank You, Lord today...

Thank You, Lord today...

Thank you Lord that there is never a shortage of words in my mouth. The gift of gab is a grand gift that eats up a great deal of time and energy. But through those words I learn about others and how I can serve you and them.

Lord thank you that you set my mouth into motion at the beginning of the day and shut it at the end.

Thank you for water, inspiring soda and hot steaming coffee on a cold day.

Thank you that you offer me the words to minister to other people's hearts.

I love you.

Watch the way you talk. Let nothing foul or dirty come out of your mouth. Say only what helps, each word a gift.
Ephesians 4::29 (MSG)

Thank You, Lord

Thank You, Lord today...

71

Thank You, Lord today...

Thank you Lord that you are the faithful fingerprint that identifies me as one-of-a-kind and special to you.

You are always there in the midst of my troubles, waiting for me to call your Holy name. Thank you Father that you make things happen. Thank you that you understand me, and that you allow me to understand you much more intimately so it may become routine for me to lay down my feeble mind and body before you. Oh, how I do want to lay down my life and completely follow you.

Thank you for that desire, it is my heart I love you, Lord.

> Before a word is on my tongue
>   you, Lord, know it completely.
> You hem me in behind and before,
>   and you lay your hand upon me.
> Such knowledge is too wonderful for me,
>   too lofty for me to attain.
>   Psalm 139: 4-6 (NIV)

Thank You, Lord

Thank You, Lord today...

Thank You, Lord today...

Thank you that you are awesome and that I am able to be in your magnificant world for even just a second to admire your incredible work. Your creativity is striking and your versatility amazes my humble mind.

Lord, thank you that I am not you, that I need you, that you created me with both free will and loving dependence in mind. You authored in me a serendipitous poem that lives each day curious to know you more, to see more, to praise more and more as I experience the world around me.

I love you Lord.

Be cheerful no matter what; pray all the time; thank God no matter what happens. This is the way God wants you who belong to Christ Jesus to live.

Thessalonians 5: 17-18

Thank You, Lord

Thank You, Lord today...

Thank You, Lord today...

Thank you for reminding me of your wonderful promises; for my eternal salvation through Jesus Christ and for helping me to feel your love in the deepest depths of my soul.

Thank you for helping me to treat those whom my human side dispises with your utmost and tender care.

Thank you for helping me to turn to those who have hurt me so deeply and remind them that the well of your love is still full and waiting for them to partake.

Thank you for giving me patience Lord; for giving me love Lord; for giving me the right frame of mind to carry through my darkest nights. You are faithful dear God.

Thank you.

Jesus said, Everyone who drinks this water will get thirsty again and again. Anyone who drinks the water I give will never thirst not ever. The water I give will be an artesian spring within, gushing fountains of endless life.
John 4:14 (MSG)

Thank You, Lord

Thank You, Lord today...

Thank You, Lord today...

Thank You, Lord today...

Thank You, Lord today...

Month 2

Thank You, Lord today...

Thank You God that You are faithful to me everyday. You are always there in the midst of my troubles, waiting for me to call Your Holy name.

Thank You Father that You make things happen, both good and bad.

Thank You that You understand me and allow me to understand myself more intimately every day.

Please make it commonplace for me to lay down my feeble mind and body for You. Oh, how I do want to lay down my life and completely follow you.

I love You, Lord.

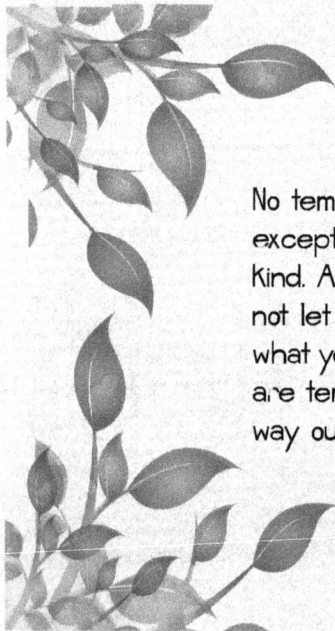

No temptation has overtaken you except what is common to man-kind. And God is faithful: he will not let you be tempted beyond what you can bear. But when you are tempted, he will also provide a way out so that you can endure it.
1 Corinithians 10: 13 (NIV)

Thank You, Lord

Thank You, Lord today...

Thank You, Lord today...

Thank You, Lord for special people who sand rough edges off my life, those You bless with the ability to create joy and laughter; who foster strength and honor; who emanate courage and protection.

Thank You for giving those people funny accents and perfect timing and a few extra dollars to give away when they are really needed.

Thank You for the experience of knowing and loving those special people and for letting them rub off on me in the most peculiar and wonderful of ways.

They are Your special blessing.

I love You, Lord.

—•❀•—

As iron sharpens iron, so one person sharpens another.

Proverbs 27:17 (NIV)

Thank You, Lord

Thank You, Lord today...

Thank You, Lord today...

Thank You that I am Your clay, that I am molded, little by little into the spirit that You so intimately desire me to be.

Push me from my comfort zone and shave away the unkind edges of my personality.

Thank You Lord that I am not in charge of Your miraculous world; the one that no man can completely discover or explain; the world that You took seven days to create and more than 2,000 years to nurse along.

Yet you, Lord, are our Father. We are the clay, you are the potter; we are all the work of your hand

Isaiah 64: 8. (NIV)

Thank You, Lord

Thank You, Lord today...

Thank You, Lord today...

Thank You, Lord that You are present and powerful today, tomorrow and for eternity.

Lord teach me that I am not You, that I need You, that a willing heart and willing dependence is what You had in mind when You created me.

Remind me of Your wonderful promises for my eternal salvation through Jesus Christ. Help me feel Your love in the deepest depths of my soul.

Thank You that You help me to treat those whom my human side dispises with Your utmost and tender care. Thank You that I can turn to those who have hurt me so deeply and remind them that the well of Your love is still full and waiting for them to partake.

Love must be sincere. Hate what is evil; cling to what is good.
Romans 12: 9 (NIV)

Thank You, Lord

Thank You, Lord today...

Thank You, Lord today...

Thank You, Lord that You give me patience, love and the right frame of mind to carry through my darkest nights.

You are faithful dear God.

You are always faithful to those who love You.

Thank You that I can see a glimpse of heaven when I search Your Word and allow Your Spirit to change my heart.

I love You, Lord Thank You.

However, as it is written: What no eye has seen, what no ear has heard, and what no human mind has conceived, the things God has prepared for those who love him; these are the things God has revealed to us by his Spirit.

1 Corinthians 2: 9-10

Thank You, Lord

Thank You, Lord today...

Thank You, Lord today...

Thank You Lord for simple pleasures that make life a joy to live.

Thank You for the little smiles, the little jokes that tickle my throat and make me feel like I'm going to laugh out loud.

Thank You Lord for the funny words that explode from my children's mouths at appropriate and inappropriate times.

Thank You for their stories that make me laugh with heartfelt joy and think about things that I would not have otherwise thought about.

Thank You for open hearts that care enough to care for me.

Worship the Lord with gladness;
come before him with joyful songs.
Psalm 100 1:2 (NIV)

Thank You, Lord

Thank You, Lord today...

Thank You, Lord today...

Thank You Lord for blessing me with the eternal promise that You are my Shepherd. You look out for me when I am scared and cowering in the clouded darkness of fear. You carry my weight, burdens and all, through every kind of trial I encounter.

Thank You Lord for blessing me with the promised help of the Holy Spirit.

You said in Your Word that You would send a helper to be with Your children, and You did.

Comfort and peace in You shall I have in my heart all the days of my life. Thank You, Lord.

Praise be to the God and Father of our Lord Jesus Christ, the Father of compassion and the God of all comfort, 4 who comforts us in all our troubles, so that we can comfort those in any trouble with the comfort we ourselves receive from God.

2 Corinthians 1 :3 and 4 (NIV)

Thank You, Lord

Thank you, Lord today...

Thank You, Lord today...

Thank You Lord for blessing me with the realization that no material thing carries the importance of You.

It is the treasure of Your Word, the understanding of its meaning, the encouragement of the Holy Spirit that I want in my life.

No price could be attached to the riches You've given freely, no value assessable for the price You paid in order to give them.

Thank You, Lord that You give me that gift freely and offer the same gift to anyone who wants it.

Thank You, Lord.

Hide me from the conspiracy of the wicked, from the plots of evildoers.
Psalm 64: 2 (NIV)

Thank You, Lord

Thank You, Lord today...

Thank You, Lord today...

Thank You Lord for heavenly peace that truly does pass all understanding.

Thank You that in Your infinate wisdom You are leading Your children through a wilderness of strange and awkward experiences that only You fully comprehend.

But the irony of it all Lord is that to You there is no wilderness, no prairie or frontier awkward or foreign.

Thank You Lord for designing my life map.

Thank You for Your constant attention to my journey and Your persistence to teach me the lessons You need me to know.

For I know the plans I have for you, declares the Lord, plans to prosper you and not to harm you, plans to give you hope and a future.

Jeremiah 29: 11 (NIV)

Thank You, Lord

Thank You, Lord today...

Thank You, Lord today...

Thank You for inspiring me to new heights of joy.

Little things, Lord.

It's the little things that remind me of Your omniscent presence.

Thank You Lord You cause the sun to rise and the sea to ebb and flow.

Thank You Lord You cause the moon to twirl around the great galaxy of stars and the heavens to peak through the sky and into my heart.

Thank You Lord You make the rain fall on the parched unhappy skin of the desert.

Thank You Lord that You don't give up.

I love You Lord.

I form the light and create darkness, I bring prosperity and create disaster; I, the Lord, do all these things.
                    Isaiah 45: 7 (NIV)

100   Thank You, Lord

Thank You, Lord today...

101

Thank You, Lord today...

Thank You Lord for those precious nuggets of golden knowledge that help me know Your will.

Thank You that You are a mightly and glorious Lord.

Thank You for loving me. When on my knees, humbled by my arrogance and dead in my sins, I asked you to live in my heart and You moved in and bleached my crimson heart.

Joy is my treasure and the hard roads are made easier.

Thank You, Lord that I cried and You were close. Your knowledge and wisdom made me wonder why I ever committed such injustices against myself by living without You.

I love You Lord.

Then the Lord God formed a man from the dust of the ground and breathed into his nostrils the breath of life, and the man became a living being.

Genesis 2: 7 (NIV)

102

Thank You, Lord

Thank You, Lord today...

Thank You, Lord today...

Thank You Lord for Your undeniable movement among those who truly love You.

Thank You Lord that You answer prayers in a mighty way and bring smiles to those who are burdened by the weight of the world, swimming in grief, stunned by a diseased world.

Thank You that Your wonderful will always ends in praise, Your insightful plan always ends in honor. Thank You Lord for the hard and most painful times that produce the overhwelming joy that You so genrously pour over the hearts of Your servants. Lord, Your hand is swift and Your patience is perfectly counted. I love You, Lord.

Restore to me the joy of your salvation and grant me a willing spirit, to sustain me.
Psalm 51: 12 (NIV)

Thank You, Lord

Thank You, Lord today...

Thank You, Lord today...

Thank You Lord that when I
am troubled You provide just
the right person to call and
say just the right thing.
Thank You Lord that
when I am down, You,
through your Holy
Spirit, help me find
guidance and hope.
Thank You Lord
that when I am angry
You soften the fire
that burns out of
control in me.
Thank You, Lord.
I love You.

... because human anger does not
produce the righteousness that
God desires.

James 1: 20 (NIV)

Thank You, Lord

Thank You, Lord today...

Thank You, Lord today...

Thank You Lord that You never leave me alone. Thank You that You gave me children and family and friends with whom I can share my burdens, fears, joys and experiences.

Thank You that You gave me Your Word.

Your listening ear and Your Holy Spirit guide me through my decisions.

Thank You Lord that You keep Your promises. You promised me great riches in You.

Thank You Lord, that I am rich indeed.

Do not store up for yourselves treasures on earth, where moths and vermin destroy, and where thieves break in and steal.

Matthew 6: 19 (NIV)

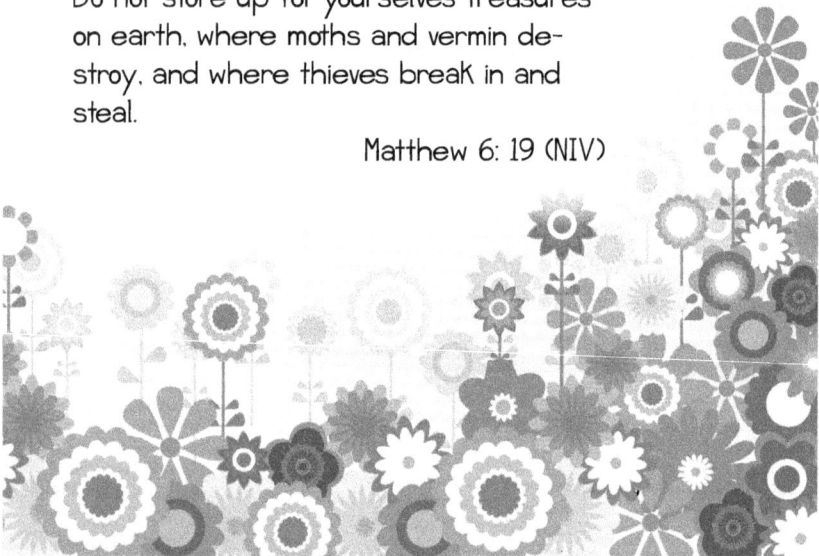

Thank You, Lord today...

Thank You, Lord today...

Thank You Lord for providing new days for me to enjoy. Thank You for new weeks, new months, new years and even new millenniums over time.

The world turns at Your command.

The sun rises and sets as You deem fit.

Thank You Lord that we humans are not in charge of ceasing society as we know it.

Thank You that You alone are in charge of our destiny.

You alone know the day, the hour and the minute of Your return.

You are prepared for every event and happening that will take place before Your chosen time.

Thank you that we are not able to end it ourselves, but that You alone are in ultimate control.

So you also must be ready,
because the Son of Man will
come at an hour when you
do not expect him.
                    Matthew 24:44 (NIV)

Thank You, Lord

Thank You, Lord today...

Thank You, Lord today...

Thank You Lord that You never turn Your face from me, even when I dissapoint You through my sinful nature.

Father You are a loving God and You are a caring God and You are an eternal God.

Thank You Lord that You are the God of Abraham, the God of Jacob, the God of Issac and the God of me.

I love You, Lord.

... for all have sinned and fall short of the glory of God.
Romans 3: 23 (NIV)

Thank You, Lord

Thank You, Lord today...

Thank You, Lord today...

Thank You Lord that today's outlook is brighter than yesterday's.

Thank You Lord that as the days pass, my outlook grows brighter still.

Lord even in my darkest hours You shine a light in my heart by way of the Holy Spirit that proivdes me with warmth, joy and Your perfect will.

Thank You Lord that You bless me with love, peace, patience, kindness, goodness, gentleness, faithfulness and self control.

I love You, Lord.

●—●🅑●—●

But the fruit of the Spirit is love, joy, peace, forbearance, kindness, goodness, faithfulness, gentleness and self-control.

Galatians 5: 22 and 23 (NIV)

Thank You, Lord

Thank You, Lord today...

Thank You, Lord today...

Thank You Lord for supplying my needs: Both emotional and physcial.
You send just the right people to aid with notes and words of encouragement and love. They are more important than money.
You, God, love me. Thank you Lord for giving me life.
I love You.

Command those who are rich in this present world not to be arrogant nor to put their hope in wealth, which is so uncertain, but to put their hope in God, who richly provides us with everything for our enjoyment. Command them to do good, to be rich in good deeds, and to be generous and willing to share. In this way they will lay up treasure for themselves as a firm foundation for the coming age, so that they may take hold of the life that is truly life.

1 Timothy 6: 17-19 (NIV)

Thank You, Lord

Thank You, Lord today...

Thank You, Lord today...

Thank You, Lord that You died to bridge the enormous gap created by my sins.

It was through Your death that I was invited to share eternal life. That gift is too often said without thought and too often pondered without action.

You moved my heart, made me the person I am inside and out. Thank You that everyone can choose to receive Your love and understand the sacrifce You made on our behalf.

I love You Lord.

For this is what the Lord says he who created the heavens, he is God; he who fashioned and made the earth, he founded it; he did not create it to be empty, but formed it to be inhabited he says: I am the Lord, and there is no other.

Isaiah 45:18 (NIV)

Thank You, Lord

Thank You, Lord today...

Thank You, Lord today...

Thank You Lord for Your continual provisions for me and my family.

Before the sun rises each morning, I am laden with a gloomy cloud of debt and burden.

But without fail, every sunrise brings with it another promise that You are there, You will provide for my needs.

Thank You Lord that Your love for me is complete. You have given me a foundation to stand on that is solid and pure.

You have given me guidance through your living Word. You have blessed me with Christian brothers and sisters who are by my side.

Thank You Lord.

And I will ask the Father,
and he will give you another
advocate to help you and be
with you forever.
John 14:16 (NIV)

Thank You, Lord

Thank You, Lord today...

Thank You, Lord today...

Thank You Lord for Your resounding voice that moves in the heart of Your humbled servant.

Thank You that You tell me how to act and show me how to respond through your Word.

Thank You Lord that You lovingly pick me up by the shoulder straps and place me back on the track of righteousness.

All Scripture is God-breathed and is useful for teaching, rebuking, correcting and training in righteousness, so that the servant of God may be thoroughly equipped for every good work.
2 Timothy 3: 16 and 17 (NIV)

Thank You, Lord

Thank You, Lord today...

Thank You, Lord today...

Thank You for listening to the call of my heart and not the voice of my critics. Thank You that You are a perfect judge and You call to my mind the sins I need to confess.

Thank You that You care so much for me that You would hang around when all others think of me as mud. Thank You that You dry the tears of my eyes and replace my sadness with joy through other servants You call to my side.

Flee the evil desires of youth and pursue righteousness, faith, love and peace, along with those who call on the Lord out of a pure heart.

2 Timothy 2: 22 (NIV)

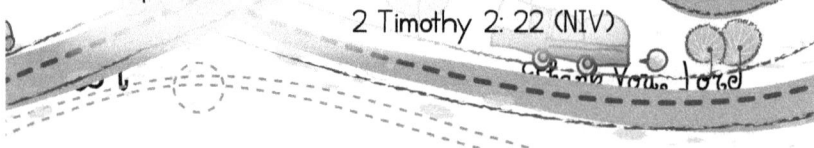

Thank You, Lord today...

Thank You, Lord today...

Thank You Lord for accepting me dirty; for cleaning my pores of the rot and grit that the world carves into me.

Thank You for understanding that I am simply human and that though I desire perfection, I am not perfect. I desire endless service to Your kingdom, but I tire. Thank You, Lord that You understand. When I desire to live in Your Holy likeness, it is only because of Your holiness mirrored in me. Thank You, Lord. I love You.

If anyone has material possessions and sees a brother or sister in need but has no pity on them, how can the love of God be in that person?

1 John 3: 17 (NIV)

Thank You, Lord

Thank You, Lord today...

Thank You, Lord today...

Thank You, Lord, for the debilitating death of my ego-centric dreams.

I know You have more important things for me to do.

Thank You, Lord, for making my life hard, for forcing me out of my comfort zone, for molding me, the hard way, into the servant You truly desire me to be.

Thank You that You are in charge of my life Lord, and considering all the confusing twists and turns it takes every day,

I love You.

Love is patient, love is kind. It does not envy, it does not boast, it is not proud. It does not dishonor others, it is not self-seeking, it is not easily angered, it keeps no record of wrongs. Love does not delight in evil but rejoices with the truth. It always protects, always trusts, always hopes, always perseveres.

1 Corinthians 4: 7-13 (NIV)

Thank You, Lord

Thank You, Lord today...

Thank You, Lord today...

    Thank You, Lord, for teaching me how to diffuse the hate of others with love sent directly from You.
    What a wonderful tool Your heavenly love is Lord, and, I love to see that when unleashed, it swirls with power and majesty.
    Thank You, Lord, for being sovereign, Holy, ever-present and all I need, Lord.

> If I speak in the tongues of men or of angels, but do not have love, I am only a resounding gong or a clanging cymbal.
> 1 Corinthians 13: 1 (NIV)

Thank You, Lord

Thank You, Lord today...

Thank You, Lord today...

Thank you for your smooth hand that rubs my sore bones and heals my broken heart.

Thank you for your wise mind that decides justly what should happen to me.

Thank you for your deep, unfathomable love that permeates this earth and reminds even the hardest of hearts that you are the one and only Almighty God.

I love you, Lord.

———•ß•———

Trust in the Lord with all
your heart, and do not lean
on your own understanding.
Proverbs 3:5 (ESV)

Thank You, Lord today...

Thank You, Lord today...

Thank You, Lord, for the worst days of my life;
the ones that pierce my soul and impale my heart.

Only You, Lord, can ease my grief and sorrow.

Thank You, Lord, for the most devastating failures
I've ever experienced.

It reminds me that I am human and You are God.

Thank You, Lord, for the fragile condition of earthly
things. My reliance on them is too strong, my reliance on
You, Lord, is weak.

Godly sorrow brings
repentance that
leads to salva-
tion and leaves no
regret, but worldly
sorrow brings death.
2 Corinthians 7: 10
(NIV)

Thank You, Lord

Thank You, Lord today...

Thank You, Lord today...

Thank you Lord for Your powerful voice that tells me its all right and knows that it truly is.

Thank You for being my Savior in my hour of need and in my moments of discontent.

Lord, I am humbled by Your power and mercy, and embarrassed by Your insistance to be faithful to me, Your lost lamb.

Thank You, Lord for being a true friend and for sacrificing Yourself as the perfect example for me to follow.

I love You Lord.

He put a new song in my mouth, a
hymn of praise to our God.
Many will see and fear the Lord and
put their trust in him.

                    Psalm 40: 3 (NIV)

Thank You, Lord

Thank You, Lord today...

Thank You, Lord today...

Thank You, Lord, that You are ever so patient in waiting for me to find my way to Your side; ever so eager to see me complete Your will; ever so pleased when I do what's right.

Thank You that Your voice wafts into my ears and reminds me of Your present love, Your past love, and Your future love for me and my siblings.

Lord, I am weak. Thank You for being strong. I am scared. Thank You for being secure. I am troubled. Thank You for being stable. I don't know what I'd do to get through this test called life without You.

Thank You for being God, that I don't have to try to be God myself. I love You, Lord.

Sing to God, sing in praise of his name, extol him who rides on the clouds; rejoice before him his name is the Lord.

Psalm 68: 4

Thank You, Lord today...

Thank You, Lord today...

Thank You, Lord, that in my desperation You are the steel beam of my salvation and Your strong arms are the truss of my life.

Thank You, Lord for Your glorious promise that no matter where I walk, You are there.

Thank You, Lord that You are the guide who leads me when I walk into the deep woods of despair.

●—●ᗷ●—●

And now what are you waiting for? Get up, be baptized and wash your sins away, calling on his name.

Acts 22: 16 (NIV)

Thank You, Lord

Thank You, Lord today...

Thank You, Lord today...

I love You, Lord. You are the open arms that love me when I can't love myself. Thank You, Lord.

Thank You, Lord, for protection in Your tumultuous world.

Thank You, Lord that when the earth trembles Lord, You are in control.

When it moans, You yearn to satisfy its cravings. When it shakes violently, Lord, You move Your hand into action.

I love your power Lord.

I love you.

.. for it is God who works in you to will and to act in order to fulfill his good purpose.

Philippians 2:13 (NIV)

142

Thank You, Lord

Thank You, Lord today...

Thank You, Lord today...

Thank You, Lord, for Your awesome wonder.

Thank You that every now and then You send something or someone along to remind me of Your completely unfathomable, humanly uncontrollable, totally unpredictable power.

Thank You that You are my shelter when life's worst storms hover overhead.

You remind me Lord of the painstaking efforts You put into commanding the sun to rise and sending the moon aloft in the sky each night.

Thank You, Lord that I can enjoy your gifts.

I love You Lord.

For the Spirit God gave us does not make us timid, but gives us power, love and self-discipline.
2 Timothy 1: 7 (NIV)

Thank You, Lord

Thank You, Lord today...

Thank You, Lord today...

Thank You, Lord

Thank You, Lord today...

Thank You, Lord today...

Thank You, Lord

www.ingramcontent.com/pod-product-compliance
Lightning Source LLC
LaVergne TN
LVHW041321080426
835513LV00008B/540